MOTIVATION

INSPIRATION BOOK 101

Get Off Your Ass And Start Working On Your Wildest Dreams

Julius Hunter

Table of Contents

Chapter 1:

Taking Action Is The Only Cure To Laziness

Action is the key to manifesting your dreams into reality.

First it must be built in the mind,

Then the body must take action to build it in the world.

You can't get going until you get going.

Laziness is holding you back.

You can't start successful,

but you can't be successful until you start.

Laziness is a sign of low self-esteem.

You don't do it because you don't believe you can.

You fear taking a leap of faith that is necessary for your success.

Take action towards the goal,

however small the progress is.

Reading a book on the subject for an hour a day,

exercising for an hour a day

will both bring you closer to your physical and emotional goals.

Most people underrate themselves.

What if all people were similar and could achieve similar results with similar effort?

Think about that.

Is that not reality?

If we agree it is, we have all sold ourselves short and it becomes clear we could be far more.

People would not be lazy if they knew they could do it for sure.

The truth is you have as much chance of being successful as Richard Branson or Opera Winfrey.

Andrew Carnegie, founder of U.S steel who was one of the richest people in history started as a poor Scottish mill worker.

He also gave away all his wealth in old age through philanthropy.

An important example of character for anyone.

Opportunity was a lot harder to find back then.

Your odds are far better today.

He had to sail across the world and spend decades building a company from nothing.

Today it is entirely possible to become successful without even leaving your home.

From your phone you can conduct business worldwide.

Laziness is simply a symptom of low faith in one's self.

As Henry Ford famously said.

" Weather you think you can, or think you can't , you are right.".

I believe this to be as true today as it was then.

The result is totally dependent on what you think.

If you think you can't, that is the problem.

The symptom is laziness and the result is nothing.

Not even failure, because failure would require effort and laziness is the lack of effort.

The curse of laziness is far worse than failure.

Those who fail can hold their heads high knowing they tried.

Those who fail by default due to laziness will taste the sour taste of true regret,

never knowing if they could have won because they never played.

Action is the only cure for laziness.

By taking the first step towards the goal,

you will see that this step brings progress.

It will motivate you to take the next step,

building momentum towards your goal.

Laziness is linked to self-esteem and your beliefs.

It can be overcome when you change your believes about yourself and your situation.

Take the first step of action when you don't feel ready is the leap of faith.

Without summoning the courage to take this leap we cannot fly.

Just as in nature,

if you were to base jump off a cliff,

your suit does not allow you to glide immediately,

first you must drop so the wind can catch your suit.

It's just the same in life.

As you take your leap,

things will often get worse before they get better.

To help the wind catch your suit you must continue to take action away

from the cliff, because if you stay still and hit the rocks your dream will

not catch the wind and die.

Keeping moving always

Look for the next step and continue towards the beautiful flight ahead.

Keeping in mind your inner concept of the dream,

of soaring on life's breeze,

living the high life with ease.

If the why for your end result is big enough,

it will give you the courage to take the leap and withstand the drop.

Always with the most magnificent image of your future life at the

forefront of your mind,

keep unwavering faith that this is going to happen for you.

Through taking constant action,

having a burning desire for success,

there will be no room for laziness in your life.

Once you have taken the leap and endured the drop,
nothing will stop you from gliding from success to success.
But you must act now for success waits for no one.

Chapter 2:

There's No Time for Regrets

Regret. Guilt. Shame.

These are three of the darkest emotions any human will ever experience. We all feel these things at different points in our lives, especially after making a "bad" decision. There are certain situations some of us would rewind (or delete) if we could. The reality is, however, there is an infinite number of reasons we should never regret any of the decisions we make in our lives.

Here are 7 of them:

1. Every decision allows you to take credit for creating your own life.

Decisions are not always the result of thoughtful contemplation. Some of them are made on impulse alone. Regardless of the decision, when you made it, it was something you wanted, or you would not have done it (unless someone was pointing a gun at your head).

Be willing to own the decisions you make. Be accountable for them. Take responsibility and accept them.

2. By making any decision involving your heart, you have the chance to create more love in the world by spreading yours.

Your love is a gift.

Once you decide to love, do it without reservation. By fully giving of yourself, you expand your ability to express and receive love. You have added to the goodness of our universe by revealing your heart to it.

3. By experiencing the disappointment that might come with a decision's outcome, you can propel yourself to a new level of emotional evolution.

You aren't doing yourself any favors when you try to save yourself from disappointment. Disappointment provides you with an opportunity to redefine your experiences in life. By refining your reframing skills, you increase your resilience.

4. "Bad" decisions are your opportunity to master the art of self-forgiveness.

When you make a "bad" decision, *you* are the person who is usually the hardest on yourself. Before you can accept the consequences of your decision and move on, you must forgive yourself. You won't always make perfect choices in your life. Acknowledge the beauty in your human imperfection, then move forward and on.

5. Because of the occasional misstep, you enable yourself to live a Technicolor life.

Anger. Joy. Sadness.

These emotions add pigment to your life. Without these things, you would feel soulless. Your life would be black and white.

Make your decisions with gusto. Breathe with fire. You are here to live in color.

6. Your ability to make a decision is an opportunity to exercise the freedom that is your birthright.

How would you feel if you had no say in those decisions concerning your life? Would you feel powerless? Restricted? Suffocated?

Now, focus on what it feels like to make the decisions you want to make. What do you feel? Freedom? Liberty? Independence?

What feelings do you *want* to feel?

Freedom. Liberty. Independence.

As luck would have it, the freedom you want is yours. Be thankful for it in every decision you make, "good" or "bad."

7. When you decide to result in ugly aftermath, you refine what you *do* want in your life.

It's often impossible to know what you want until you experience what you don't want. With every decision, you will experience consequences.

Use those outcomes as a jumping-off point to something different (and better) in your future.

Chapter 3:

What To Do When You Feel Like Giving Up

I remember going through the phase when I saw nothing but black. When nothing seemed to cheer me up. When even the calmest of breeze shook me off my feet. But I can also tell that I am not in that place now.

I can understand and feel the pain that most people go through. The common pain of not knowing what to do with life when we are at the bottom of that well.

We get stuck at the bottom because we have had our fair share of failures. I know we don't get enough chances to give things the right twist. So we are open to using the chances when we deem necessary.

No matter how hard we try, we always get hit back harder, because we are being tested in the hardest ways out there. We need to do some things on our own because life might not cooperate with us.

You might have heard the phrase, 'Every Action has an Equal and opposite reaction'. I know it I a scientific fact, but it is also a fact about life. Let me explain.

Whenever we try to create a new path, or we try to create a new thing, a thing that never existed before that, nature acts against it and tries to normalize it. This act of nature creates a conflict and it appears to us as if everything is acting against us.

That everything wants us to stop. That everything wants us to fail. That everyone wants you to remain the same. And that is when you feel like giving up.

I know this all sounded silly. But I wanted to make you realize that everything happens for a reason. And I wanted you to realize that finding this story stupid means that at least now you are trying to follow reason and make a logical explanation for everything that happens to you.

But now if you want to find a reason, let me give you one. You are being tested because if you give up now, then you don't have a good enough reason to live for. But if you decide to keep the struggle going, then you have a reason to live for and you are motivated enough to keep the life cycle going.

This reason on its own is a worthy cause to keep going. You can find yourself stuck in the deepest darkest corner of your life but you must always find a way to climb up. Because you had a reason for all your actions when you first started and those reasons have not changed.

The reasons might have faded away because you wanted to follow an easy path. But the path is never easy. It never was and it never will be. It might be shorter sometimes and sometimes it might take your whole life to finish it. But you will always need to keep going along it because this is the purpose of your life that you yourself have set.

Chapter 4:

Why You Are Amazing

When was the last time you told yourself that you were amazing? Was it last week, last month, last year, or maybe not even once in your life?

As humans, we always seek to gain validation from our peers. We wait to see if something that we did recently warranted praise or commendation. Either from our colleagues, our bosses, our friends, or even our families. And when we don't receive those words that we expect them to, we think that we are unworthy, or that our work just wasn't good enough. That we are lousy and under serving of praise.

With social media and the power of the internet, these feelings have been amplified. For those of us that look at the likes on our Instagram posts or stories, or the number of followers on Tiktok, Facebook, or Snapchat, we allow ourselves to be subjected to the validation of external forces in order to qualify our self-worth. Whether these are strangers who don't know you at all, or whoever they might be, their approval seems to matter the most to us rather than the approval we can choose to give ourselves.

We believe that we always have to up our game in order to seek happiness. Everytime we don't get the likes, we let it affect our mood for the rest of the day or even the week.

Have you ever thought of how wonderful it is if you are your best cheerleader in life? If the only validation you needed to seek was from yourself? That you were proud of the work you put out there, even if the world disagrees, because you know that you have put your heart and soul into the project and that there was nothing else you could have done better in that moment when you were producing that thing?

I am here to tell you that you are amazing because only you have the power to choose to love yourself unconditionally. You have the power to tell yourself that you are amazing. and that you have the power to look into yourself and be proud of how far you came in life. To be amazed by the things that you have done up until this point, things that other people might not have seen, acknowledged, or given credit to you for. But you can give that credit to yourself. To pat yourself on the back and say "I did a great job".

I believe that we all have this ability to look inwards. That we don't need external forces to tell us we are amazing because deep down, we already know we are.

If nobody else in the world loves you, know that I do. I love your courage, your bravery, your resilience, your heart, your soul, your commitment, and your dedication to live out your best life on this earth. Tell yourself each and everyday that you deserve to be loved, and that you are loved.

Go through life fiercely knowing that you don't need to seek happiness, validations, and approval from others. That you have it inside you all along and that is all you need to keep going.

Chapter 5:

The Power of Contentment

Today we're going to talk about why contentment is possibly a much more attainable and sustainable alternative than trying to achieve happiness.

Happiness is a limited resource that needs energy and time to build, and we can never really be truly happy all the time. But what about the notion of contentment?

Contentment is a state of feeling that you are satisfied with the current situation and it need not go beyond that. When we say we are contented with our circumstances, with our jobs, with our friends, family, and relationships, we are telling ourselves that we have enough, and that we can and should be grateful for the things we have instead of feeling lacking in the things we don't.

Many a times when i ask myself if i am happy about something, be it a situation that I had found myself in, or the life that I am living, majority of the time the answer is a resounding no. And it is not because I am unhappy per se, but if i were to ask myself honestly, I can't bring myself to say that yes absolutely that all is great and that I am 100$% truly happy with everything. I have to say that this is my own personal experience and it may not be an accurate representation of how you see life.

However, if i were to reframe and ask myself this question of "Am I Contented with my life?" I can with absolute confidence say yes I am. I may not have everything in the world, but i can most definitely say I am contented with my job, my friends, my family, my career, my relationships, and my health and body. That I do not need to keep chasing perfection in order to be contented with myself.

You will find that as you ask yourself more and more if you are contented, and if the answer is mostly a yes, you will gradually feel a shift towards a feeling that actually life is pretty good. And that your situation is actually very favourable. Yes you may not be happy all the time, but then again who is? As long as you are contented 90% of the time, you have already won the game of life. And when you pair contentment with a feeling of gratefulness of the things you have, you will inevitably feel a sense of happiness without having to ask yourself that question or be trying to chase it down on a daily basis.

Many a times when I looked at my current situation to see if I was on the right track, I look around me and I feel that whilst there may be areas that I am lacking and certainly needs improvement, in the grand scheme of things, I am pretty well off and i am contented.

So I challenge all of you today to look at your life in a different perspective. Start asking yourself the right question of "are you contented", and if by any chance you are not majority of the time, look at what you can do to change things up so that you do feel that life is indeed great and worth living.

Chapter 6:

Why You're Demotivated By A Values Conflict

Every human being, in fact, every organism in this universe is different from even the same member of their species. Every one of us has different traits, likes, dislikes, colors, smells, interests so it's natural to have a difference of opinion.

It's natural to have a different point of view. It's natural and normal to have a different way of understanding. And it's definitely normal for someone else to disagree with your ways of dealing with things.

Most of us don't want to see someone disagreeing with us because we have this tricky little fellow inside of us that we call EGO.

Our ego makes us feel disappointed when we see or hear someone doing or saying something better than us. We cannot let go of the fact that someone might be right or that someone might be Okay with being wrong and we can't do a single thing about it.

This conflict of values occurs within ourselves as well. We want to do one thing but we cannot leave the other thing as well. We want to have something but we cannot keep it just because we don't have the resources to maintain them.

This feeling of 'want to have but cannot have' makes us susceptible to feelings of incompleteness ultimately making us depressed. The reality of life is that you can't always get what you want. But that doesn't make it a good enough reason to give up on your dreams or stop thinking about other things too.

Life has a lot to offer to us. So what if you can't have this one thing you wanted the most. Maybe it wasn't meant for you in the first place. Nature has a way of giving you blessings even when you feel like you have nothing.

Let's say you want something but your mind tells you that you can't have it. So what you should do is to find alternative ways to go around your original process of achieving that thing and wait for new results. What you should do is to give up on the idea altogether just because you have a conflict within your personality.

You cannot let this conflict that is building within you get a hold of you. Clear your mind, remove all doubts, get rid of all your fears of failure or rejection, and start working from a new angle with a new perspective. Set new goals and new gains from the same thing you wanted the first time. This time you might get it just because you already thought you had nothing to lose.

This feeling of 'No Regret' will eventually help you get over any situation you ever come across after a fight with your inner self. This feeling can help you flourish in any environment no matter what other people say or do behind your back.

Nothing can bring you peace but yourself. Nothing holds you back but your other half within you.

Chapter 7:

The Difference Between Professionals and Amateurs

It doesn't matter what you are trying to become better at. If you only do the work when you're motivated, then you'll never be consistent enough to become a professional. The ability to show up every day, stick to the schedule, and do the work, especially when you don't feel like it — is so valuable that you need to become better 99% of the time. I've seen this in my own experiences. When I don't miss workouts, I get in the best shape of my life. When I write every week, I become a better writer. When I travel and take my camera out every day, I take better photos. It's simple and powerful. But why is it so difficult?

The Pain of Being A Pro

Approaching your goals — whatever they are — with the attitude of a professional isn't easy. Being a pro is painful. The simple fact of the matter is that most of the time, we are inconsistent. We all have goals that we would like to achieve and dreams that we would like to fulfill, but it doesn't matter what you are trying to become better at. If you only do the work when it's convenient or exciting, then you'll never be consistent enough to achieve remarkable results.

I can guarantee that if you manage to start a habit and keep sticking to it, there will be days when you feel like quitting. When you start a business, there will be days when you don't feel like showing up. When you're at the gym, there will be sets that you don't feel like finishing. When it's time to write, there will be days that you don't feel like typing. But stepping up when it's annoying or painful or draining to do so, that's what makes the difference between a professional and an amateur.

Professionals stick to the schedule. Amateurs let life get in the way. Professionals know what is important to them and work towards it with purpose. Amateurs get pulled off course by the urgencies of life. **You'll Never Regret Starting Important Work.**

Some people might think I'm promoting the benefits of being a workaholic. "Professionals work harder than everyone else, and that's why they're great." That's not it at all.

Being a pro is about having the discipline to commit to what is important to you instead of merely saying something is important to you. It's about starting when you feel like stopping, not because you want to work more, but because your goal is important enough to you that you don't simply work on it when it's convenient. Becoming a pro is about making your priorities a reality.

There have been many sets that I haven't felt like finishing, but I've never regretted doing the workout. There have been many articles I haven't felt like writing, but I've never regretted publishing on schedule. There have been many days I've felt like relaxing, but I've never regretted showing up and working on something important to me.

Becoming a pro doesn't mean you're a workaholic. It means that you're good at making time for what matters to you — especially when you don't feel like it — instead of playing the role of the victim and letting life happen to you.

Chapter 8:

<u>Meditate For Focus</u>

Meditation calms the mind and helps you to focus on what is important. It dims the noise and brings your goals into clearer vision.

Meditation has been practised as far back as 5000bc in India - with meditation depicted in wall artisan from that period.
That is 1500 years older than any written artefact ever found.
It is as old as the archaeological evidence of any human society.

Meditation can change the structure of the brain promoting focus, learning and better memory, as well as lowering stress and reducing the chances of anxiety and depression.

Whilst there are many different types and ways to meditate,
the ultimate goal is to clear your mind and calm your body
so that you can focus on your dream.
Aim to look inward for answers.
It could be aided by music relating to your dream or videos.
The music, the images, and imagining you are already living that life will bring it into reality.

Your mind creates the vision and the feeling
in your heart will bring it to you.

When your mind and heart work together it creates balance,

leading to happiness and success.

Meditation is the process of bringing the

visions of the mind and the desires of the heart together,

which in turn will form your life.

Meditation clears all the threats to this -

such as worry and distraction.

It will bring you clear focus and open up the next steps in your journey.

Meditation is often best done when you first wake or before you go to

sleep, but it can be incorporated into your day.

If clear consistent thought brings decisive action and success,

it is important to dwell on your dreams as often as possible.

Calm your mind of the unnecessary noise that is robbing you of your

focus.

The more realistic you make this vision

and the more you feel it in your heart,

the quicker it will come.

Meditation can help you achieve this

whether you follow a guide or make it up yourself.

The key is calm and focus.

Your subconscious knows how to get there.

Meditation will help open up that knowledge.

Science is just beginning to unlock the answers on why meditation is so effective, even so it has been used for over 7000 years to help people relax and focus on their goals.

The positive health and well-being evidence of meditation is well documented.

We may not yet understand it fully,

But just know that it works and use it every day.

You don't need to understand every detail to use something that works.

Meditation is perhaps one of the most time tested tools in existence.

It could work for you, if you try it.

It could change your life forever.

Chapter 9:

Your Mind is A Suggestion Engine

What we go through each day and what we want every day is what our mind wants us to think and believe.

Let's just think about, whatever you are doing right now apart from reading this post. Something your mind came up with by making a reasonable argument with you.

So what you have in your mind right now, is your reality. You have memories of your past that are related to actual people and places that you have encountered or been to in your life.

So you go in that place of your mind where you have to be in charge of what to feel right now. But it's not you who wants to be in charge, it's your brain that is the one dictating you.

It's not wrong to say that your conscious mind is your master. The mind is the master of the body.

If at any time in your life you feel lost and have a breakdown, where you don't have a solution for your current problems, just pause for a moment. Give your mind some time to try out new things and it will certainly push you new ideas.

There is no feasible problem that you cannot solve. You only need to give the problem and your mind some time to familiarize and you will surely get the best possible solution and the easiest way out.

If at any time you decide to pull out, just stay put and give your mind a moment. It will make you visualize the things you will miss out on and the things that you wouldn't be able to achieve if you don't go after them.

Your life is the sum total of all your positive and negative thoughts. If you keep having negative thoughts it means you have equipped your mind with things that you shouldn't have. It means that you are not giving your mind enough space to generate newer and better thoughts and ideas for you to work on.

The harder you concentrate on your failures, the more chance you have to get stuck. Stuck in a place where neither your brain nor your body is teaming up with your fate.

So you have to be cautious of what you want to believe in and what you want to pursue in your leisure time. Because if you cannot control that suggestion engine on top, then you would surely have a dismal life and it won't be anyone else's fault.

If you want a day full of happy thoughts and feelings, you have to try to replace any negative thought that comes up in your mind with not one but two happy thoughts.

You yourself have to create your own reality that you live in. For that, you have to train your mind. Train it in such a way that you can generate an array of wild yet soothing, comforting, and loving thoughts. That promotes you to go the extra mile and live like a whole and a new Human Being.

You can do anything, just till you keep facing your fears and having an acceptance of them.

Chapter 10:

Share Your Wisdom with the World

Today we're going to talk about how to share your wisdom with the world. How many of you think that you have something meaningful to share with others? Whether you are an expert at a particular field, or just that you are particularly good at a certain task.

Have you ever thought about putting your knowledge out there so that people can learn from you?

It is incredibly powerful the gifts that you and I possess. We all have different talents, wisdom, knowledge, that are unique to each individual. No 2 humans are the same, and that goes the same for what they have to offer. What you have to give is uniquely special to you and you only.

I want to bring light to this topic because I too was once afraid to let my voice be heard. I felt that I had no authority, certification, or whatever qualification to be able to write on relationships or about life. I always thought that what I had to say maybe wasn't that important, that it wouldn't help anybody. But i soon realized that it was my own limiting beliefs about myself that were holding me back from sharing my truth with the world.

As I leaned in to more about personal development, I opened my eyes to the wonderful possibilities that we all have to offer as humans. I started to believe that maybe I had something worth sharing. That maybe an article that i wrote or a video that i put out, or an audiobook that i published could help someone somewhere, somehow.

I started to believe that as long as I can change 1 life, that would be good enough a reason for me to spend my time and energy into publishing something that would go out there into the world. Yeah there will be haters. Yes there will be people telling me that what I say is stupid or doesn't make sense, but as long as I believed in what i had to say, it was all that mattered.

We all have a right to share our truth. That truth may not sit well with everyone, but you will find your audience. If you have something to say, put it out there. Help someone in need.

Social media and the internet has become such a powerful force that everything we share can be instantaneously broadcasted all over the world. Think of that kind of power. If you have a powerful voice, a positive one, share it.

that is my challenge for each and everyone of you today. To believe in yourself, your wisdom, and not be afraid to show it to the world.

Chapter 11:

Share Your Troubles Freely and Openly

Life is hard. We go through tons of challenges, problems, and obstacles every single day. We accumulate problems and stresses left right and Center. Absorbing each impact blow for blow.

Over time, these impacts will wear us down mentally and physically. Without a proper release channel, we find that our emotions spill over in ways when we least expect it. We get easily irritated, have a hard time falling asleep, have mood issues, and find ourselves even being temporarily depressed at times.

When we bottle negativity, it festers inside us without us realising what we have done. That is where releasing those tensions by pouring our heart and soul into friends, writing, journaling, and other outlets that allow us to express our feelings freely without judgement.

We may not all have friends that we can truly count on to share our deepest darkest secrets for fear that they might share these secrets unsuspectingly. If we do have these types of friends, treasure them and seek them out regularly to share your problems. By bouncing ideas off someone, we may even find a new solution to an old problem that we couldn't before. The other party may also be able to see things more objectively and with a unique perspective that is contrary to yours which you could potentially use to your advantage.

If writing things down is something that helps you cope with life, then by all means take a piece of paper and write down all the things that have been bothering you. Journal it, archive it. You may even write a song about it if that helps you process things better. Writing things down help us clear our minds and lets us see the big picture when we come back to it at a later date should we feel ready to address it. When things are too crazy, we may not have the mental capacity to handle everything being thrown at us at one go. So take the time to sort those feelings out.

You may also choose to just find a place that brings you relaxation. Whether it be going to the beach, or renting a hotel, or even just screaming at the top of your lungs. Let those feelings out. Don't keep it hidden inside.

IF all these things still don't work for you, you may want to try seeking help from a professional counsellor or therapist who can work out these issues you have in your life one by one. Never be afraid to book an appointment because your mental health is more important than the stigma associated with seeing a professional. You are not admitting you have a problem, you are simply acknowledge that there are areas in your life that you need assistance with. And that it is perfectly okay and perfectly normal to do so. Counsellors have the passion to serve, the passion to help, and that is why they chose that profession to being with. So seek their assistance and guidance as much as you need to.

Life isn't easy. But we can all take a conscious effort to regulate our emotions more healthily to live a long and balanced life.

Chapter 12:

Playing To Your Strengths

Have you ever asked yourself why you fail at everything you touch?

Why you seem to lack behind everyone you strive to beat?

Why you can't give up the things that are keeping you from achieving the goals you dream?

Has anyone told you the reason for all this?

You might wonder about it all your life and might never get to the right answer. Even though you stare at the answer every day in the mirror.

Yes! It's you! You are the reason for your failures.

You are the reason for everything bad going on in your life right now.

But you are also the master of your life, and you should start acting like one.

When the world brings you down, find another way to overcome the pressures.

Find another way to beat the odds.

Adverse situations only serve to challenge you.

Be mentally strong and bring the world to your own game.

Show the world what you are.

Show the world what you are capable of.

Don't let anyone dictate to you what you should do.

Rather shape your life to dictate the outcome with your efforts and skills.

You can't always be wrong.

Somewhere, and somehow, you will get the right answer.

That will be your moment to build what you lost.

That will be your moment to shut everyone else and rise high in the silence of your opponents.

If you don't get that chance, don't wait for it to come.

Keep going your way and keep doing the things you do best.

Paths will open to your efforts one day.

You can't be bad at everything you do.

You must be good at something.

Find out what works for you.

Find out what drives your spirit.

Find out what you can do naturally while being blind-folded with your hands tied behind your back.

There is something out there that is calling out to you.

Once you find it, be the best at it as you can.

It doesn't matter if you do not get to the top.

You don't anything to prove to anyone.

You only need one glimpse of positivity to show yourself that you have something worthwhile to live for.

Always challenge yourself.

If you did 5 hours of work today, do 7 tomorrow.

If you run 1 mile today, hit 3 by the end of the week.

You know exactly what you are capable of.

Play to your strengths.

Make it your motto to keep going every single day.

Make a decision.

Be decisive.

Stick with it.

Don't be afraid because there is nothing to fear.

The only thing to fear is the fear itself.

Tell your heart and your mind today, that you can't stop, and you won't stop.

Till the time you have the last breath in your lungs and the last beat in your heart, keep going.

You will need to put your heart out to every chance you can get to raise yourself from all this world and be invincible.

You have no other option but to keep going.

To keep trying until you have broken all the barriers to freedom.

You are unique and you know it.

You just need to have the guts to admit that you are special and live up to the person you were always meant to be.

Take stock of yourself today.

Where are you right now and where do you want to be?

The moment you realize your true goal, that is the moment you have unlocked your strengths.

Live your life on your terms.

Every dream that you dream is obtainable.

And the only way is to believe in yourself.

To believe that you are the only thing standing in the way of your past and your future.

Once you have started, tell yourself that there is no return.

Dictate your body to give up only when you have crossed the finish line.

Start acting on every whim that might get you to the ultimate fate.

These whims are your strength because you have them for a purpose.

Why walk when you can run?

Why run when you can fly?

Why listen when you can sing?

Why go out and dine when you can cook?

The biggest gift that you can give to yourself is the mental satisfaction that you provide yourself.

You are only limited to the extent you cage yourself.

The time you let go will be your salvation. But you have to let go!

Chapter 13:

Overcoming Tiredness and Lethargy

Tiredness and lethargy has become a major problem for youths and adults these days. As our lives get busier and our ability to control our sleep gets more out of hand, we all face a constant struggle to stay alert and engaged in our life's work every single day. And this problem hits me as well.

You see, many of us have bad sleep habits, and while it might feel good to stay up late every night to watch Netflix and binge on YouTube and Instagram posts, we pay for it the next day by being a few hours short of a restful night when our alarm wakes us up abruptly every morning.

We tell ourselves that not needing so much sleep is fine for us, but our body tells us a different story. And we can only fake being energetic and awake for so long. Sooner or later we will no doubt experience the inability to function on an optimal level and our productivity and mood will also be affected accordingly. And this would also lead to overall tiredness and lethargy in the long run.

Before we talk about what we can do to counter and fix this problem that we have created for ourselves, we first have to understand why we consciously allow ourselves to become this tired in the first place.

I believe that many of us choose entertainment over sleep every night is because we are in some ways or another overworked to the point that we don't have enough time to ourselves every single day that we choose to sacrifice our sleep time in order to gain back that few hours of quality personal time. After spending a good 10 hours at our jobs from 9-6pm, and after settling down from the commute home and factoring in dinner time, we find ourselves with only a solid 1-2 hours of time to watch our favourite Netflix shows or YouTube, which i believe is not very much time for the average person.

When presented with the choice of sleep versus another episode or two of our guilty pleasure, it becomes painfully obvious which is the "better" choice for us. And we either knowingly or unknowingly choose entertainment and distraction over health.

Basically, I believe the amount of sleep you choose to give yourself is directly proportionate to how happy you are about your job. Because if you can't wait to get up each and everyday to begin your life's work, you will give yourself the best possible sleep you can each night to make sure you are all fired up the next day to crush your work. But conversely, if you hate your job and you feel like you have wasted all your time at work all day, you will ultimately feel that you will need to claim that time back at night to keep yourself sane and to keep yourself in the job no matter how much you dislike it. Even if it means sacrificing precious sleep to get there.

So I believe the real question is not how can we force ourselves to sleep earlier every night to get the 8 hours of sleep that we need in order not to feel tired and lethargic, but rather is there anything we can change about how we view our job and work that we come home at the end of the day feeling recharged and fulfilled to the extend that we don't have to look for a way to escape every night into the world of entertainment just to fill our hearts.

When you have found something you love to do each day, you will have no trouble going to bed at 10pm each night instead of 1 or 2am.

So I challenge each and everyone of you to take a hard look at WHY you are not getting enough sleep. There is a high chance that it could boil down to the reason I have described here today, and maybe a change in careers might be something to consider. But if you believe that this tiredness and lethargy is born out of something medical and genetic, then please do go see a doctor to get a medical solution to it.

Otherwise, take care and I wish you all the best in reclaiming back your energy to perform at your peak levels of success. See you in the next one.

Chapter 14:

Why You're Demotivated By Lack of Clarity

Clarity is key to achieving any lasting happiness or success.

Demotivation is almost certain without clarity.

Always have a clear vision of what you want and why you want it.

Every detail should be crystal clear as if it were real.

Because it is.

Mustn't reality first be built on a solid foundation of imagination.

Your skills in visualisation and imagination must be strong to build that foundation.

You must build it in the mind and focus on it daily.

You must believe in it with all your heart and your head will follow.

Create it in the mind and let your body build it in reality.

That is the process of creation.

You cannot create anything in reality without clarity in the mind.

Even to make a cup of coffee, you must first imagine making a cup of coffee.

It doesn't take as much clarity as creating an international company, but focus and clarity are required nonetheless.

The big goals often take years of consistent focus, clarity and commitment.

That is why so few succeed.

Demotivation is a symptom of lack of direction.

To have direction you must have clarity.

To have clarity you must have a clearly defined vision of you future.

Once you have this vision, never accept anything less.

Clarity and vision will begin your journey,

but your arrival depends on stubbornness and persistence.

Before you start you must decide to never quit, no matter what happens.

Clarity of your why will decide this for you.

Is the pain you are about to endure stronger than your reasons?

If you are currently demoralised by lack of clarity,

sit down and decide what will really make you happy.

Once you have decided, begin to make it feel real with pictures around your house.

Listen to motivational music and speeches daily to build your belief in you.

Visit where you dream you will be one day.

Get a feel for your desired new life.

Create actions that will build clarity in your vision.

Let it help you adjust to your new and future reality.

Slowly adjust your vision upwards.
Never adjust downwards.
Never settle for less.

The more real your vision feels the more likely it will be.
Begin to visualise living it.
Before long you will be living it.

Adopt the mannerisms of someone who would be in that position.
When you begin to believe you are important, others will follow.
Carry yourself like a champion.
Soon you will be one.

Have clarity you have about who you are.
Have clarity about what you are going to do.
Motivate yourself to success.

Once you step on that path you will not want to return to the you of yesterday.
You will be committed to becoming even better tomorrow.
You will be committed to being the new person you've always known you could be.

Always strive to get another step closer to your vision.
Work until that vision becomes clearer each day.

Have faith that each week more opportunities for progression will present themselves to you.

Clarity is the key to your success.

Chapter 15:

How To Find Motivation

Today we're going to talk about a topic that hopefully will help you find the strength and energy to do the work that you've told yourself you've wanted or needed to but always struggle to find the one thing that enables you to get started and keep going. We are going to help you find motivation.

In this video, I am going to break down the type of tasks that require motivation into 2 distinct categories. Health and fitness, and work. As I believe that these are the areas where most of you struggle to stay motivated. With regards to family, relationships, and other areas, i dont think motivation is a real problem there.

For all of you who are struggling to motivate yourself to do things you've been putting off, for example getting fit, going to the gym, motivation to stay on a diet, to keep working hard on that project, to study for your exams, to do the chores, or to keep working on your dreams... All these difficult things require a huge amount of energy from us day in and day out to be consistent and to do the work.

I know... it can be incredibly difficult. Having experienced these ups and downs in my own struggle with motivation, it always starts off swimmingly... When we set a new year's resolution, it is always easy to think that we will stick to our goal in the beginning. We are super motivated to go do the gym to lose those pounds, and we go every single day for about a week... only to give up shortly after because we either don't see results, or we just find it too difficult to keep up with the regime.

Same goes for starting a new diet... We commit to doing these things for about a week, but realize that we just simply don't like the process and we give up as well...

Finding motivation to study for an important exam or working hard on work projects are a different kind of animal. As these are things that have a deadline. A sense of urgency that if we do not achieve our desired result, we might fail or get fired from our company. With these types of tasks, most of us are driven by fear, and fear becomes our motivator... which is also not healthy for us as stress hormones builds within us as we operate that way, and we our health pays for it.

Let's start with tackling the first set of tasks that requires motivation. And i would classify this at the health and fitness level. Dieting, exercise, going to the gym, eating healthily, paying attention to your sleep... All these things are very important, but not necessarily urgent to many of us. The deadline we set for ourselves to achieve these health goals are arbitrary. Based on the images we see of models, or people who seem pretty fit around us, we set an unrealistic deadline for ourselves to achieve those body goals. But more often than not, body changes don't happen in days or weeks for most of us by the way we train. It could take up to months or years... For those celebrities and fitness models you see on Instagram or movies, they train almost all day by personal trainers. And their deadline is to look good by the start of shooting for the movie. For most of us who have day jobs, or don't train as hard, it is unrealistic to expect we can achieve that body in the same amount of time. If we only set aside 1 hour a day to exercise, while we may get gradually fitter, we shouldn't expect that amazing transformation to happen so quickly. It is why so many of us set ourselves up for failure.

To truly be motivated to keep to your health and fitness goals, we need to first define the reasons WHY we even want to achieve these results in the first place. Is it to prove to yourself that you have discipline? Is it to look good for your wedding photoshoot? Is it for long term health and fitness? Is it so that you don't end up like your relatives who passed too soon because of their poor health choices? Is it to make yourself more attractive so that you can find a man or woman in your life? Or is it just so that you can live a long and healthy life, free of medical complications that plague most seniors by the time they hit their 60s and 70s? What are YOUR reasons WHY you want to keep fit? Only after you know these reasons, will you be able to truly set a realistic deadline for your health goals. For those that are in it for a better health overall until their ripe old age, you will realize that this health goal is a life long thing. That you need to treat it as a journey that will take years and decades. And small changes each day will add up. Your motivator is not to go to the gym 10 hours a day for a week, but to eat healthily consistently and exercise regularly every single day so that you will still look and feel good 10, 20, 30, 50 years, down the road.

And for those that need an additional boost to motivate you to keep the course, I want you to find an accountability partner. A friend that will keep you in check. And hopefully a friend that also has the same health and fitness goals as you do. Having this person will help remind you not to let yourself and this person down. Their presence will hopefully motivate you to not let your guard down, and their honesty in pointing out that you've been slacking will keep you in check constantly that you will do as you say.

And if you still require an additional boost on top of that, I suggest you print and paste a photo of the body that you want to achieve and the idol that you wish to emulate in terms of having a good health and fitness on a board where you can see every single day. And write down your reasons why beside it. That way, you will be motivated everytime you walk past this board to keep to your goals always.

Now lets move on to study and work related tasks. For those with a fixed 9-5 job and deadlines for projects and school related work, your primary motivator right now is fear. Which as we established earlier, is not exactly healthy. What we want to do now is to change these into more positive motivators. Instead of thinking of the consequences of not doing the task, think of the rewards you would get if you completed it early. Think of the relief you will feel knowing that you had not put off the work until the last minute. And think of the benefits that you will gain... less stress, more time for play, more time with your family, less worry that you have to cram all the work at the last possible minute, and think of the good results you will get, the opportunities that you will have seized, not feeling guilty about procrastinations... and any other good stuff that you can think of. You could also reward yourself with a treat or two for completing the task early. For example buying your favourite food, dessert, or even gadgets. All these will be positive motivators that will help you get the ball moving quicker so that you can get to those rewards sooner. Because who likes to wait to have fun anyway?

Now I will move on to talk to those who maybe do not have a deadline set by a boss or teacher, but have decided to embark on a new journey by themselves. Whether it be starting a new business, getting your accounting done, starting a new part time venture.. For many of these tasks, the only motivator is yourself. There is no one breathing down your neck to get the job done fast and that could be a problem in itself. What should we do in that situation? I believe with this, it is similar to how we motivate ourselves in the heath and fitness goals. You see, sheer force doesn't always work sometimes. We need to establish the reasons why we want to get all these things done early in life. Would it be to fulfil a dream that we always had since we were a kid? Would it be to earn an extra side income to travel the world? Would it be to prove to yourself that you can have multiple streams of income? Would it to become an accomplished professional in a new field? Only you can define your reasons WHY you want to even begin and stay on this new path in the first place. So only you can determine why and how you can stay on the course to eventually achieve it in the end.

Similarly for those of you who need additional help, I would highly recommend you to get an accountability partner. Find someone who is in similar shoes as you are, whether you are an entrepreneur, or self-employed, or freelance, find someone who can keep you in check, who knows exactly what you are going through, and you can be each other's pillars of support when one of you finds yourself down and out. Or needs a little pick me up. There is a strong motivator there for you to keep you on course during the rough time.

And similar to health and fitness goal, find an image on the web that resonates with the goal you are trying to achieve. Whether it might be to buy a new house, or to become successful, i want that image to always be available to you to look at every single day. That you never forget WHY you began the journey. This constant reminder should light a fire in you each and everyday to get you out of your mental block and to motivate you to take action consistently every single day.

So I challenge each and every one of you to find motivation in your own unique way. Every one of you have a different story to tell, are on different paths, and no two motivators for a person are the same. Go find that one thing that would ignite a fire on your bottom everytime you look at it. Never forget the dream and keep staying the course until you reach the summit.

Chapter 16:

Feeling That You Don't Have Enough Time

Today we're going to talk about a topic that I think many of us struggle with, myself included. The topic is about feeling that we don't have enough time to do the things that we need to do.

Personally I feel this one a daily basis, and it is partly because of my expectations versus reality. Many a times I set unrealistic expectations of how much time is required to do a particular task on my list that I tend to pack my schedule with way too many items. This leads me to feeling incredible overwhelm and stress because it just doesn't seem like I can get all my objectives down before 12am. We tend to underestimate the amount of time and energy that working on our goals require of us that many times we end up setting ourselves up for failure.

I would watch the clock go by minute by minute, hour by hour, only to find myself still working on the very first task on my list of 10 things to do. As you can already imagine I end up feeling that I'm not being productive, even though most of the time I am, and this feeling that I'm not doing things fast enough erodes my motivation further.

There are times when I am genuinely unproductive - like when I get lost in watching television, browsing the web, playing with my dog, being distracted for the sake of procrastination, and a myriad of reasons. But for the purposes of this topic, I will not be addressing those issues. I want to turn our attention to what we can actually accomplish if given enough time, assuming our level of productivity isnt affected by distractions.

The first thing we have to realise is that the things that we need to get done will take however long it needs to get done. Many times we may not be able to control or accurately measure the duration that a task may take. Instead of setting a time limit on a task, we should instead measure our productivity and be focused on doing rather than completing.

As an entrepreneur, I've come to learn that my work never ends. When I think I have finished one task, another one just comes crashing onto my desk like a meteor - another fire I have to put out, another problem I have to solve. I've come to realise that once I set a deadline for the time I need to complete something, rarely will I ever get it done on time. Most often I will be off by a long shot - either by the hours or even days.

Instead of setting arbitrary number of hours, I found that what worked best for me was to simply let my productivity flow. That I actually do more and accomplish more when I stop worrying about time itself - that I give my work however long it needs to get done and then call it a day.

This has allowed me to not be stressed that I never feel like I don't have enough time. Because in reality, time is relative. Time is something that I assign meaning to. If I simply focus on my designation, my 10 year plan, all I need to do is to simply work hard each day and that'll be good enough for me.

Right now the only thing that makes me feel like I don't have enough time, is when I actually waste them doing nothing meaningful. Having struggled with procrastination all my life, I've come to find out that I am not an innate workaholic. It doesn't come natural to me to want to do the work and that is what is causing me to feel like time is slipping away from me sometimes. That is something I have to continuously work on.

With regards to what you can learn from this - instead of racing against time to complete something, let the work flow out of you like water. Get into a state where productivity oozes out of you. Use a time tracking app to measure the amount of time that you have spent on working. Decide how much time you are willing to set aside to do your work and commit to that time. If 8 hours is the ideal, ensure that you clock those 8 hours and then end the day proud of yourself that you had already done what you set out to do at the start of the day. Never feel like you must do more and never beat yourself up for it. Be nicer to yourself as life is already hard enough as it is.

Another tip that I can recommend that has worked for me is to set a list of the top 3 things you want to do at the start of your day. Instead of the 10 that I did previously that caused me so much stress and anxiety, I have found that 3 is the ideal number of things that will bring us the most satisfaction and the least overwhelm when completing. If we are not able to complete those 3 big tasks, at least maybe we have done 1 or 2. We won't beat ourselves that we hadn't done those other 8 things at the back.

If on the other hand we have successfully completed all those 3 things by mid-day, we may choose to add another 3 items on our list. That way the carrot is never too far away and it is easily attainable should we want to add more.

So I challenge each and everyone of you to look into your day with a new set of lens. Set your intentions right at the start of each day and focus on productivity on a focused set of 3 items. Let the work flow out of you and let the task complete its course naturally without rushing. Remember that it will take as long as it takes and you will only bring yourself more stress if you set a deadline on it. Use it only as a tool for motivation but nothing else if you must set a deadline. Don't be too hard on yourself. Focus on the journey and don't be overly stressed out by feeling that you're always racing against time.

Chapter 17:

Confidence: The Art of Humble-Pride

There is a very fine line between confidence and overconfidence, being bold and being belligerent, having authority and having arrogance. It is a line that trips even the most nimble footed, but usually because they have dedicated no clear thoughts on how to manage it. Instead, they follow their gut on how far they can push or how much they should hold back. This is the paradox; you need to be confident. You need self-belief, you need to be assured of your ability and sometimes even certain of what the outcome will be. All of those things are empowering. In the words of Tony Robbins, you have to awaken the giant within. But had Goliath stooped to consider David's sling he would have worn a different helmet. The problem was that Goliath had a belief that he was fully capable of everything just as he was. I like to call it confidence without context, or universal, unanimous support of the self. That is the dangerous kind of confidence that spills over into arrogance. Chess grandmasters will tell you that the moment you assume you will win is the moment you lose. Because that is precisely when you start to make mistakes. You become too focussed on what your next move is that you don't even see theirs. You become so absorbed in your strategy that you fail to account for their plan and the bigger picture. It was confidence without context that made Goliath run straight towards to the flying stone.

Confidence without context is an assumption. And the problem with assumptions is that they go one step beyond the rationality of an expectation. Assumption goes into the fight drunk, having already celebrated the victory. But that leads to its inevitable demise. Expectation remains present, it acknowledges the reality of the situation. Assumption arrives intoxicated, expectation arrives in control. That is the difference. Pride is the greatest antidote to reason, which makes humility its greatest ally. If you want to stay in the fight you need to have both confidence and humility. If you want to stay competitive, if you want to get a promotion, if you want to level up. Whatever it is that you want, I can guarantee that the path to get there is a hopscotch of humility and confidence. Every bold step forward must be followed by a humble one. Note that humility does not take you backwards, it keeps you balanced. You can hop along in arrogance, but you will never last as long or be as strong as the one who keeps an even stride. If you strive for something, then you need to start striding towards it. And the rhythm of your march should beat to the sounds of a two-tone drum. Because confidence without context is like hopping up stairs – you might reach the second floor, but you will never manage the pyramid.

Chapter 18:

How To Rid Yourself of Distraction

Distraction and disaster sound rather similar.

It is a worldwide disorder that you are probably suffering from.

Distraction is robbing you of precious time during the day.

Distraction is robbing you of time that you should be working on your goals.

If you don't rid yourself of distraction, you are in big trouble.

It is a phenomenon that most employees are only productive 3 out of 8 hours at the office.

If you could half your distractions, you could double your productivity.

How far are you willing to go to combat distraction?

How badly do you want to achieve proper time management?

If you know you only have an hour a day to work, would it help keep you focused?

Always focus on your initial reason for doing work in the first place.

After all that reason is still there until you reach your goal.

Create a schedule for your day to keep you from getting distracted.

Distractions are everywhere.

It pops up on your phone.

It pops up from people wanting to chat at work.

It pops up in the form of personal problems.

Whatever it may be, distractions are abound.

The only cure is clear concentration.

To have clear concentration it must be something you are excited about.

To have clear knowledge that this action will lead you to something exciting.

If you find the work boring, It will be difficult for you to concentrate too long.

Sometimes it takes reassessing your life and admitting your work is boring for you to consider a change in direction.

Your goal will have more than one path.

Some paths boring, some paths dangerous, some paths redundant, and some paths magical.

You may not know better until you try.

After all the journey is everything.

If reaching your goal takes decades of work that makes you miserable, is it really worth it?

The changes to your personality may be irreversible.

Always keep the goal in mind whilst searching for an enjoyable path to attain it.

After all if you are easily distracted from your goal, then do you really want it?

Ask yourself the hard questions.
Is this something you really want? Or is this something society wants for you?

Many people who appear successful to society are secretly miserable.
Make sure you are aware of every little detail of your life.
Sit down and really decide what will make you happy at the end of your life.

What work will you be really happy to do?
What are the causes and people you would be happy to serve?
How much money you want?
What kind of relationships you want?
If you can build a clear vision of this life for you, distractions will become irrelevant.
Irrelevant because nothing will be able to distract you from your perfect vision.

Is what you are doing right now moving you towards that life?
If not stop, and start doing the things what will.
It really is that simple.

Anyone who is distracted for too long from the task in hand has no business doing that task. They should instead be doing something that makes them happy.

We can't be happy all the time otherwise we wouldn't be able to recognize it.

But distraction is a clear indicator you may not be on the right path for you.

Clearly define your path and distraction will be powerless.

Chapter 19:

Do You Know What You Want?

Do you know who you are? Do you know what you are? Do you know what you want to become? Do you have any idea what you might become?

Every sane human has asked these questions to themselves multiple times in their lives. We have a specific trait of always finding the right answers to everything. We humans always try to find the meaning behind everything.

It's in our built-in nature to question everything around us. Yet we are here in this modern era of technology and resources and we don't have a sense of purpose. We don't have a true set of goals. We don't give enough importance to our future to take a second and make a long-term plan for longer gains.

The fault in our thinking is that we don't have a strict model of attention. We have too many distractions in our lives to spare a moment to clear our minds.

The other thing that makes us confused or ignorant is the fact that people have a way of leading us into thinking things that are not ours to start with.

Society has made these norms that have absolutely nothing to do with anyone except that these were someone's experience when they were once at our stage. We are dictated on things that are not ours to achieve but only a mere image of what others want us to achieve or don't.

No one has the right to tell you anything. No one has a right to say anything to you except if they are advising or reminding you of the worst. But to inflict a scenario with such surety that it will eventually happen to you because you have a fault that many others had before you is the most superstitious and illogical thing to do on any planet let alone Earth.

No one knows what the future holds for anyone. No one can guarantee even the next breath that they take. So why put yourself under someone else's spell of disappointment? Why do you feel the need to satisfy every person's whim? Why do you feel content with everyone around you getting their ways?

You always know in your heart, deep down in some corner what you want. You will always know what you need to be fulfilled. You will always find an inspiration within yourself to go and pursue that thing. What you need are some self-confidence and some self-motivation. You need to give yourself some time to straighten up your thoughts and you will eventually get the BOLD statement stating 'This is what I want'.

You don't need to shut everyone around you. You just need to fix your priorities and you will get a vivid image of what things are and what they can become.

There is no constraint of age or gender to achieving anything. These are just mental and emotional hurdles that we have imposed on our whole race throughout our history.

Just remember. When you know what you want, and you want it bad enough to give away everything for that, you will someday find a way to finally get it.

Chapter 20:

Friendship The Key To Happiness

Today we're going to talk about the power of friendship and why i believe everyone needs to have at least 1 or 2 close friends in their lives to make life actually meaningful and worth living.

You see, for many years while i was working hard towards my goals, i spent almost all of my time on my business and little to zero time on building Long lasting relationships. And this one sided approach to success left me with a hole that weakened me emotionally, but also physically as well.

In this very myopic view of what I felt success should be and what I felt i needed to do at that point, I prioritised my career first over everything else, neglecting my own personal health, family, and friends. Whenever I was invited for a meal or an outing I always declined, viewing that it was a waste of time. That it was taking time away from my work that i should be focusing on. And as I declined more and more of these offers from friends, the invite also became less and less frequent as they saw me as someone who was either too busy, or just didn't bother to want to take this friendship to the next level.

For a while I was actually happy, that i remember telling myself that yes I dont have plans for the week and that i can focus on my work wholeheartedly. But what i failed to realise was that I was prioritise making money over everything else. And that i was losing the connection with other humans. I started to become more withdrawn, more introverted, and I was losing that spark that i once had when conversing with friends. I wasn't experiencing life enough to have any meaningful moments that I could look back on and say that wow those were great times.

It all became one giant blur and 3 years later, it felt truly pointless. I found myself lonely and without someone I could talk to. I even neglected my best friend to the point that we drifted so far apart that she found other people to confide into. This left me with a sinking feeling that I had failed to prioritise The people around me.

And from that point on I knew i needed to change. I knew i needed to put myself out there once again and shift my priorities to the things that truly mattered. Friends that could ask you out for a quick meal so that you could hash out some of your grievances in life, friends that you can share your happiness as well as your sadness, friends that could provide some meaning to the days you were living, and even more simply, friends that you can count on when all else fails.

You see the business that I spent 3 years building collapsed on me. And I found myself with nothing to show for it. No experiences worth highlighting. Only regrets that I had failed to put others before my selfish needs.

It was a hard climb back to establishing the friendships I once had. People had already started viewing me as a flaker and a no-show that it was now up to me to prove to them that I was open and available to be called a reliable friend once again. Some efforts on my part did not go as I had planned but I kept trying to make new connections, joining new groups, making tennis friends, starting up conversations with new people and asking if they could invite me along to an outing. And these little seeds started to show fruition. I soon found myself getting asked out for meals and games, and life started to feel a little bit better again.

After the initial struggle, the floodgates starting opening and I found myself busy with true life again, connecting with other people on a deep personal and emotional level. And i felt that that was what life was really all about. Friends that you can see yourself hanging out 40 years down the road when you are old and nobody wants you anymore.

I plan to keep sowing these seeds for as long as life allows me and I challenge each and everyone of you to do the same. Businesses and careers may not last, but hopefully the friends that you have made will.

Chapter 21:

Don't Stay At Home

Today we're going to talk about why you should consider getting out of your house as much as possible, especially if you need to get work done, or if you have some other important personal projects that requires your undivided attention to complete.

For those that work full-time jobs, we all aspire to one day be able to work from home. We all dream of one day being able to just get up from our beds and walk over to our desks to begin work.

Having tried this myself for the last 4 years, I can safely tell you that staying at home isn't all that amazing as it has been talked up or hyped up to be.

While it may sound nice to be able to work from home, in reality, distractions are tough to avoid, and procrastination is one major killer of productivity at home. Many of us have made our homes the Center of entertainment and relaxation. We buy nice couches, TVs, beds, speakers, etc, and all these items around the house are temptations for us to slack off.

For those who are living with family, or who have pets, their presence could also disrupt our productivity.

Without people around us to motivate us to keep working hard, we tend to just tell ourselves "it's okay I'll just watch this one show and then I'll get back to work", and before we know it, it is 5pm and we haven't done a single thing.

Some people love it, some people hate it, but personally, I much prefer getting my butt out of the house and into a co-working space, a cafe, or a library, where I can visually see other people working hard, which motivates me to stay away from slacking off.

Having been doing regular journaling to measure my productivity, staying at home has always resulted in my worst daily performance no matter how hard I try to make my home environment the most conducive for work. Feeling like taking nap because my bed is right there, or watching a Netflix show on my big screen tv, has always been hard to resist. You will be surprised how many hours you are potentially losing from just indulging in any of these things.

For those who really has no choice but to work from home, either to save money, or because you need to take care of a family member. I would highly suggest that you optimise your environment to give yourself the greatest chance of success.

Dedicate a room that will be made into your study/work room, ensure that there is adequate and bright lighting, and to Keep all possible distractions outside the room. Putting your work desk in your bedroom is the worst thing you can do because you will blur the lines between rest and work if you mix the two things up in one tiny space. Not only will you feel sluggish working from your bedroom, but you might also develop sleep issues as well.

Not staying at home is still your best bet for success. Find a space outside where you can be focused and have the discipline to get yourself there every single day, no matter how tired or lethargic you feel. Once you leave the house, you have already won half the battle in getting your productivity under control.

Chapter 22:

Distraction Is Robbing You

Every second you spend doing something that is not moving you

towards your goal, you are robbing yourself of precious time.

Stop being distracted!

You have something you need to do,

but for some reason become distracted by

other less important tasks and procrastinate on the important stuff.

Most people do it,

whether it's notification s on your phone or chat with colleges,

mostly less than half the working day is productive.

Distraction can be avoided by having a schedule

which should include some down time to relax

or perhaps get some of them distractions out of the way,

but time limited.

As long as everything has its correct time in

your day you can keep distraction from stealing too much of your time.

When your mind is distracted it becomes nearly impossible to

concentrate on the necessary work at hand.

Always keep this question in mind:

"is what I am about to do moving me towards my goal?"

If not, is it necessary?

What could I do instead that will?

It's all about your 24 hours.

Your actions and the reactions to your actions from that day,

good or bad.

By keeping your mind focused on your schedule that

moves you towards your goal, you will become resilient to distraction.

Distraction is anything that is not on your schedule.

You may need to alter that depending on the importance of the

intrusion.

Being successful means becoming single minded about your goal.

Those with faith do not need a plan b because they know plan A is the

only way and they refuse to accept anything else.

Any time you spend contemplating failure will add to its chances of

happening.

Why not focus on what will happen if you succeed instead?

Distraction from your vision of success is one of its biggest threats.

Blocking out distraction and keeping that vision clear is key.

Put that phone on flight mode and turn off the TV.

Focus on the truly important stuff.

If you don't do it, it will never get done.

The responsibility is all yours for everything in your life.

The responsibility is yours to block out the distractions and exercise your free-will over your thoughts and actions.

By taking responsibility and control you will become empowered.

Refuse to let anyone distract you when you're working.

Have a set time in your schedule to deal with stuff not on the schedule.

This will allow you time to deal with unexpected issues without stopping you doing the original work.

The reality is that we all only have so much time.

Do you really want to waste yours on distractions?

Do you want to not hit your target because of them?

Every time you stop for a notification on your phone you are losing time from your success.

Don't let distraction rob you of another second, minute, hour or day.

Days turn to months and months turn to years don't waste time on distractions and fears.

Chapter 23:

Achieving Happiness

Happiness is a topic that is at the core of this channel. Because as humans we all want to be happy in some way shape or form. Happiness strikes as something that we all want to strive for because how can we imagine living an unhappy life. It might be possible but it wouldn't be all that fun no matter how you spin it. However I'm gonna offer another perspective that would challenge the notion of happiness and one that maybe would be more attainable for the vast majority of people.

So why do we as humans search for happiness? It is partly due to the fact that it has been ingrained in us since young that we all should strive to live a happy and healthy life. Happiness has become synonymous with the very nature of existence that when we find ourselves unhappy in any given moment, we tend to want to pivot our life and the current situation we are in to one that is more favourable, one that is supposedly able to bring us more happiness.

But how many of us are actually always happy all the time? I would argue that happiness is not at all sustainable if we were feeling it at full blast constantly. After a while we would find ourselves being numb to it and maybe that happiness would turn into neutrality or even boredom. There were times in my life where i felt truly happy and free. I felt that i had great friends around me, life had limitless possibilities, the weather was great, the housing situation was great, and i never wanted it to end as i knew that it was the best time of my life.

However knowing that this circumstance is only temporary allowed me to cherish each and every moment more meaningfully. As i was aware that time was not infinite and that some day this very state of happiness would somehow end one way or another, that i would use that time wisely and spend them with purpose and meaning. And it was this sense that nothing ever lasts forever that helped me gain a new perspective on everything i was doing at that present moment in time. Of course, those happy times were also filled with times of trials, conflicts, and challenges, and they made that period of my life all the more memorable and noteworthy.

For me, happiness is a temporary state that does not last forever. We might be happy today but sad tomorrow, but that is perfectly okay and totally fine. Being happy all the time is not realistic no matter how you spin it. The excitement of getting a new house and new car would soon fade from the moment you start driving in it, and that happiness you once thought you associated with it can disappear very quickly. And that is okay. Because life is about constant change and nothing really ever stays the same.

With happiness comes with it a whole host of different emotions that aims to highlight and enhance its feeling. Without sadness and sorrow, happiness would have no counter to be matched against. It is like a yin without a yang. And we need both in order to survive.

I believe that to be truly happy, one has to accept that sadness and feelings of unhappiness will come as a package deal. That whilst we want to be happy, we must also want to feel periods of lull to make the experience more rewarding.

I challenge all of you today to view happiness as not something that is static and that once you achieved it that all will be well and life will be good, but rather a temporary state of feeling that will come again and again when you take steps to seek it.

I also want to bring forth to you an alternative notion to happiness, in the form of contentment, that we will discuss in the next video. Take care and I'll see you there.

Chapter 24:

How Not To Waste Your 25,000 Mornings As An Adult.

Adulthood is the time of our lives when we need to get serious about everything. We have to take care of every single thing from time to our mornings. Early morning is the time of the day when freshness consumes us—known as the best time to work. Why waste such precious time? Having a good morning automatically means having a good day too. When a mind is fresh, it works. And wasting 25,000 mornings of your adulthood would be truly foolish. Those 3571 weeks would go to waste as there was no essential work done.

To make sure that you don't waste your morning is to be sure that you have mornings. Waking up late just automatically means that half of your day has gone to waste. So, wake up early. Those early hours have some courage to work in them. And who wants to waste such an opportunity to prove themselves. Not only will it be beneficial for your professional life, but it will also be beneficial for your health. Get a decent night's sleep, and you will see the changes that come along with them.

After you open your eyes in the morning, immediately sit up. Going back to sleep is always a more intriguing option. But we need to know that our priority is to wake up. And when you are sleeping, make sure that nothing disturbs it. Phone on silent—the tv's off and lights out. Make sure you are as comfortable as possible so you won't wake up the following day grumpy. Disturbance in sleep may cause the disappearance of it. There is a chance that you can't sleep again. That is not what we want. So, we take things beforehand.

An easy way to wake up in the morning is to have some encouragement ready for you. Either it's gym or work. It will make you wake up in the morning early to jump-start whatever you have planned. Then the mornings will be a lot more efficient for you and much more enjoyable. The first thing that we tend to do right after waking up is to check our phones. We waste 20 minutes or more just lying there doing nothing much of a task. Let's get one thing clear. It's not worth it. Wake up in the morning, get a cup of coffee, and start your day without any technology, naturally.

Once you fall into a habit, you will fall into a routine. Your life will change for the good, and you will look towards the brighter side of life. Mornings are a precious time, and 25,000 of our adulthood is the most important morning of our life. So, make sure that you make every morning out of those 25,000 mornings count. It won't be easy, but it will be worth it!

Chapter 25:

Everything is A Marathon Not A Sprint

Ask your parents, what was it like to raise children till the time they were able to lift their weight and be self-sufficient. I am sure they will say, it was the most beautiful experience in their lives. But believe me, They are lying.

There is no doubt in it that what you are today is because of your parents, and your parents didn't rest on their backs while a nanny was taking care of you.

They spent countless nights of sleeplessness changing diapers and soothing you so that you can have a good night's sleep. They did that because they wanted to see a part of them grow one day and become what they couldn't be. What you are today is because of their continuous struggle over the years.

You didn't grow up overnight, and your parents didn't teach you everything overnight. It took years for them to teach you and it took even more time for you to learn.

This is life!

Life is an amalgamation of little moments and each moment is more important than the last one.

Start with a small change. Learn new skills. The world around you changes every day. Don't get stuck in your routine life. Expand your horizons. What's making you money today might not even exist tomorrow. So why stick to it for the rest of your life.

You are never too old to learn new things. The day you stop learning is the last day of your life. A human being is the most supreme being in this universe for a reason. That reason is the intellect and the ability to keep moving with their lives.

You can never be a millionaire in one night. It's a one-in-billion chance to win a lottery and do that overnight. Most people see the results of their efforts in their next generation, but the efforts do pay off.

If you want to have eternal success. It will take an eternity of effort and struggles to get there. Because life is a marathon and a marathon tests your last breaths. But when it pays off, it is the highest you can get.

Shaping up a rock doesn't take one single hit, but hundreds of precision cuts with keen observation and attention. Life is that same rock, only bigger and much more difficult.

Changing your life won't happen overnight. Changing the way you see things won't happen overnight. It will take time.

To know everything and to pretend to know everything is the wrong approach to life. It's about progress. It's about learning a little bit at each step along the way.

To evolve, to adapt, to figure out things as they come, is the process of life that every living being in this universe has gone through before and will continue to go through in the future. We are who we are because of the marathon of life.

Every one of us today has more powerful things in our possessions right now than our previous 4 generations combined. So we are lucky to be in this world, in this era.

We have unlimited resources at our disposal, but we still can't get things in the blink of an eye. Because no matter how evolved we are, we still are a slave to the reality of nature, and that reality is the time itself!

If you are taking each step to expect a treat at each stop, you might not get anything. But if you believe that each step that you take is a piece in a puzzle, a puzzle that becomes a picture that is far beautiful and meaningful, believe me, the sky is your limit.

Life is a set of goals. You push and grind to get these goals but when you get there you realize that there is so much more to go on and achieve.

Committing to a goal is difficult but watching your dreams come true is something worth fighting for.

You might not see it today, you might not see it 2 years from now, but the finish line is always one step closer. Life has always been and always will be a race to the top. But only the ones who make it to the top have gone through a series of marathons and felt the grind throughout everything.

Your best is yet to come but is on the other end of that finish line.

Chapter 26:

It's Okay To Feel Uncertain

We are surrounded by a world that has endless possibilities. A world where no two incidents can predict the other. A realm where we are a slave to the unpredictable future and its repercussions.

Everyone has things weighing on their mind. Some of us know it and some of us keep carrying these weights unknowingly.

The uncertainty of life is the best gift that you never wanted. But when you come to realize the opportunities that lie at every uneven corner are worth living for.

Life changes fast, sometimes in our favor and sometimes not much. But life always has a way to balance things out. We only need to find the right approach to make things easier for us and the ones around us.

Everyone gets tested once in a while, but we need to find ways to cope with life when things get messy.

The worst thing the uncertainty of life can produce is the fear in your heart. The fear to never know what to expect next. But you can never let fear rule you.

To worry about the future ahead of us is pointless. So change the question from 'What if?' to 'What will I do if.'

If you already have this question popping up in your brain, this means that you are already getting the steam off.

You don't need to fear the uncertain because you can never wreck your life in any such direction from where there is no way back.

The uncertainty of life is always a transformation period to make you realize your true path. These uncertainties make you realize the faults you might have in your approach to things.

You don't need to worry about anything unpredictable and unexpected because not everything is out of your control every time. Things might not happen in a way you anticipated but that doesn't mean you cannot be prepared for it.

There are a lot of things that are in your control and you are well researched and well equipped to go around events. So use your experience to do the damage control.

Let's say you have a pandemic at your hand which you couldn't possibly predict, but that doesn't mean you cannot do anything to work on its effects. You can raise funds for the affected population. You can try to find new ways to minimize unemployment. You can find alternate ways to keep the economy running and so on.

Deal with your emotions as you cannot get carried away with such events being driven by your feelings.

Don't avoid your responsibilities and don't delay anything. You have to fulfill every task expected of you because you were destined to do it. The results are not predetermined on a slate but you can always hope for the best be the best version of yourself no matter how bad things get.

Life provides us with endless possibilities because when nothing is certain, anything is possible. So be your own limit.

Chapter 27:

Live A Long, Important Life

Do you think you are more capable to deal with the failure or the regret of not trying at all?

Are you living the life you want or the life everyone else wants for you?

Would you feel good spending your time on entertainment that might not last for long? Or would you feel good feeling like you are growing and have a better self of you to look at in the mirror?

Similarly, would like to live in the present or would you love to work for a better future?

Do you want money to dictate your life or do you want money to follow you where ever you go?

Would you prefer being tired or being broke?

Do you want to spend the rest of your life in this place where you and your parents were born? Or do you won't go around the world and find new possibilities in even the most remote places?

Would you rather risk it all or play it safe?

We are often presented with all these questions in our lifetime. Most people take these questions as a way to enter into your adulthood. The answers to these questions are meant to show you the actual meaning of life.

So what is Life? Life is not your parents, your work, your friends, your events, and your functions. It's within you and around you.

You should learn to live your life to the fullest. You should love to live your life for as long as you can with a happy body and a healthy mind.

A happy and healthy body and mind are important. Because you can only feel secure on a stable platform. You can only wish to stand on a platform where you know you can stay put for a long time.

There is nothing wrong with working eight or nine hours in your daily life. It's not unhealthy or anything. Working is what gives our life a purpose. Working is what keeps us active, moving, and motivated.

We have one life, and we have to make it matter. But the way we chose to do it is what matters the most. Our choices make us who we are rather than our actions.

The life we live is the epitome of our intentions and morals. We can be defined in a single word or a single phrase if we ever try. We don't need to analyze someone else, we just need to see ourselves in the mirror and we might be able to see right across the image.

The day we are able to do that, might be the day we have actually made a worthy human being of ourselves and have fulfilled our destiny.

If you are able to look at yourself and go through your whole life in the blink of an eye and cherish the memories as if you were right there at that moment. Believe me, you have had a long and important life to make you think of it all over again every day.

Chapter 28:

Dealing With Uncertainty in Job Applications

Today we are going to touch on the topic of Job applications. While applying for jobs may be a daunting task, many a times, the wait for a response from any one of your applications may prove to be an even greater challenge. You see many of us live in fear that no one will take up on our offer to show them what we are capable of. It is not that we are lacking in any specific quality, but it is the fact that competition has become so fierce that it takes time and effort from the HR team to go through the hundreds of applications that may come in for any particular position.

Many times companies can take anywhere from 3-6 months or even longer to get back to you, or you may never even hear from them at all, which is also quite common. This does not mean you are unqualified or incapable, it just means a no for now.

The wait is always the hardest people we start to fill our minds with doubts. Doubts on whether we will ever be able to find another job again, doubts on whether we are worthy enough, doubts on whether we are capable enough, and worst of all, doubting our abilities and questioning our beliefs. Uncertainty can spiral into fear, and fear can consume us if we don't things more lightly.

So what do i suggest you do while you wait for a reply? Instead of sitting around and checking your email everyday for a potential response, why don't you go search up ways that you can make money on the side that does not require a full time job. The internet has become a powerful tool to make money, and it is a fair game that requires only your time and effort to create a business that is independent of any potential employer or HR department. You might find that learning a new skill to make money online can potentially become a part time career that you can pursue to generate income on the side while you wait for a favourable reply from a company.

Having done this myself, i have tried numerous times to apply to standard job roles that appear on job search sites. But i have found myself to be lacking in certain areas of experience that is required because I have spent most of my time after graduating college on trying to make money online. And these skills that I have acquired may not translate directly to any formal job because they are quite niche and specific. I have found however that embarking on a road less travelled has proved to be engaging and challenging at the same time.

And whilst I have still job applications that are awaiting a response, I no longer feel anxiety towards them and look forward to them as a bonus as I have build multiple side incomes that have allowed me not to lay all my eggs in one basket. This wide net that I have cast provides me with a greater sense of security and it has helped me to deal with the uncertainty of job applications greatly.

I challenge each and every one of you today to take some chances while u wait, and who knows, this part time side income that you have generate could one day overtake the salary that a standard job would ever be able to give you. Of course u can also take the time to apply for more jobs should you wish, but never just sit around and wait because waiting can be dangerous if you dont know how to manage your emotions well.

Chapter 29:

Contribute To Society In A Meaningful Way

Today we are going to talk about how and why you should do work that contributes to society in a meaningful way. And the benefits that it can bring to all aspects of your life, be it psychological, sociological, or physical.

Why do I feel that this topic is of importance that I should highlight it in today's episode? Well because if there is one thing i have noticed about my salaried friend workers around me, I do feel that they lack a bigger vision and purpose for their life. And i feel that there is a sense that the end goal of their work is not to the benefit of their own personal growth, but of the $ sign at the end. And this motivation to work towards a 5 figure pay check is one that ultimately brings not much joy and meaning to one's life.

The many friends that I have interviewed have told me repeatedly that these jobs are merely a means to an end. That it's a routine that they have pretty much resigned themselves to sustain a lifestyle that they feel is good enough for them. This mentality has gotten me to question the culture of whether a monetary goal is truly sufficient in making one truly happy. Yes to an extent, money can bring about freedom which would free up time for one to pursue their passions in life, but for most, this race towards $10k just feels futile.

I would argue that only when you know what to do with freedom of time, and that is to serve a purpose greater than your own selfish needs, can you truly have a meaningful time on this earth.

The greatest entrepreneurs today make their millions not by chasing the money per se, but rather by finding problems that they can solve. They find a gap in society, a need that needs to be filled, and invent a novel solution to a problem that aims to address those holes. Think Jeff Bezos, Steve Jobs, Elon Musk, Mark Zuckerberg. These billionaires have their customers and consumers in mind when they set out to create their mega companies that have largely dominated our world today.

Now I am not saying you need to be doing these crazy big deals to live a happy life, but i believe that everyone has an ability to start somewhere, to start small in our community. If you have no desire for entrepreneurship and are contented with being a salaried worker, that is absolutely perfect. However you can consider doing some volunteer work, and working with a community that can better the lives of someone out there even if it just by a little bit. I guarantee that these selfless acts of giving your time to help someone out in your unique way will reward you with a feeling that money just can't buy.

If you feel like you can do more, you can dedicate more of your time to a particular cause that resonates with you, that you will not feel like a chore to serve. A cause that strikes your heart and soul that makes you want to go back so that you can give more and do more.

Maybe this cause will be something you might end up dedicating your life to, you never know. But I do know that chasing money and dedicating your life to making money will never make you happy. Invest in others, invest in their spirit, invest in doing good for society will be infinitely more worthy of your time and energy.

I challenge you today to see in what areas can you contribute to society and do good for others. I believe that you will not only feel purpose, but it will help sustain you in your career and work as well, giving you a fresh perspective on what life is really all about.

Take care and see you in the next one.

Chapter 30:

Going Through Tough Times Is Part of The Journey

For someone going through tough times, for someone going through the same hardships, again and again, every day, you are trying but not getting used to all this.

Things never seem to get better and you don't think you are just right there to get a hold of things. You think you will get them this time, but they always seem to be going a new way that you never planned.

It's alright! You are not the first one to think about things this way are you certainly won't be the last one.

You are not the first person to think that you will have different achievements this time. You are not the first person to think that you will achieve bigger goals this year. You are not the first person to fail at every corner after all that determination and grit.

Life always kicks us on the blindside, and most of us know what it feels like. But not all of us want to stay in the bed all day and feel sorry for ourselves for what happened before.

People always find a way to cope with the tragedies of life. And these people know the true purpose of life. They know the true definition of life. Wanna know what that is? It's the hard times that make you a harder more precious gem.

You can never possibly understand why it is happening to you because it is what it is and you can never set your back to reality.
The reality is that no one has ever lived a reasonable life without facing the hard times. And only the people who smiled back at these hard times had a happy ending in the end.

The only thing that makes us go through life with a smile in the hope of getting a big reward at the end of it all. Our lives aren't judged on the number of success stories we write, but with the techniques, we adapt to tackle the moments when life pushes us against a wall.

It won't always be your fault but it might be your luck trying to test your limits. So why don't you show it?

Things will always go wrong in your life but that doesn't make it justifiable to put everything aside and start mourning and regretting your every mistake and every flaw. But it's time to start removing those flaws to minimize your mistakes and trying to be a perfect individual.

This is the journey to perfection that makes going through hard times justifiable. Because every stone that your pick and set aside is another hurdle being cleared for an easier road to the top.

What happens to you in life is just a glimpse of the reality, but what you do about those things in life is what living this life is actually about.

Always remember, you and your life are always like a plane. You both fly against the winds but never along it.

Chapter 31:

How To Stop Wasting Time

In the inspiring words of Marcia Wider, "It's how we spend our time here, and now, that really matters. If you are fed up with the way you have come to interact with time, change it."

Indeed, time waits for no man. The ticking of the clock should be a startling revelation to you that how precious our time on this earth is. A study conducted at the University of Calgary shows that the ratio of chronic procrastination has increased from 5% in 1978 to 26% in 2007. In other words, you don't need more time. You have to do MORE with the time you already have. Stop wasting your time on the things that don't really matter. Do you realize how many seconds and minutes and hours do we waste every day on stuff that doesn't even let us come close to reaching our goals? If you've ever come to ask yourself, "where does the time go?" then maybe you should re-think how and on what you're spending your time.

"A man who dares to waste one hour has not discovered the value of time." Charles Darwin. There are only as many as 24 hours in a day, and you've got to make sure that each of them counts for something. There's a date on the left side of the tombstone, that's the date on which you were born. When you die, another date is engraved on the right side of your tombstone, but that dash, that line that you see in the middle of both these dates, decides how much you left your mark on other people's lives as well as your own, how much you were able to impact others, that dash represents how you lived your life in the timeframe that you were given.

We all get the same amount of time. A homeless person or a beggar that wanders here and there all day brings the same amount of time as the most successful businessman. It's what we do with that time, how we presume the ticking of the clock that genuinely matters. Life flickers by us in the blink of an eye. And what do we do about that? We only give excuses and justifications. "I don't have time to go to the gym, and maybe I'll start tomorrow. I'll start studying tomorrow; one day of taking a break won't make a difference" NO! It would make all the difference in the world. Stop fearing and pitying yourself and get up. Stop wasting your time because it's a depreciating asset, and you won't get any of it back.

You have to take the first step. You can't just live your life fearing the challenges and efforts you have to put in to get somewhere higher in life. Procrastinating, watching your favorite TV show adds up to so much time, even for an hour each day. And that time is nothing but wasted. Imagine the knowledge you can gain in that one hour of each day, imagine the work that you could do, the language that you can learn, the instrument that you can learn to play. So start investing your time into something productive rather than just lying here making defenses.

"Newton's first law of productivity" states that objects at rest tend to stay at rest until they're acted upon. That book on your shelf isn't going to read itself, those weights in the gym aren't going to move by themselves, that long due essay isn't going to write itself, YOU. HAVE. TO. DO. IT! And you have to do it now. Don't wait for another hour or another day or another week; you have to take that leap of faith; you have to take that risk. Specify your days, prioritize your to-do list, eliminate all the distractions. Nothing will make you happier than knowing that you're making progress towards becoming a better version of yourself. Take breaks, but get yourself back up to your goals. Don't waste your time! "Whatever you want to do, do it now! There are only so many tomorrow's." – Pope Paul VI.

FOCUS! You should be terrified of living a life on the sidelines. Of not achieving anything whether you're 6, 16, or 60. Of doing nothing and watching the time passes by, of not making any progress and not being able to come closer to your dreams, your goals. Stop being stagnant! Start working towards your passion, your dreams, your aspirations. The separator between the people that win and lose is what we do with that time, with those seconds that we get in a day. Start working towards self-mastery, and you will begin to see the difference in all the dimensions of your life. So concentrate on developing yourself because if you don't, I guarantee you that you will make a settlement, and most people have, and most of us already have. The proper function of a man is to live, not just only to exist. We shall not waste our days trying to prolong them only, but we shall use our time effectively.

Time is free, but it's also priceless. It's perhaps the most essential commodity in this world. Once you've lost it, you can never get it back. Look back and see how many hours and days and years have you wasted doing absolutely nothing? Don't shy up from the tough things. We can't make excuses and then expect to be successful at the same time. We have to get up every day and make sure we don't quit ourselves, our goals, our dreams, our passions. Make mistakes, make them thousand times over, but make sure you learn something from every single one of them. We can't travel back to time and change the past. So don't dwell on the things that happened yesterday or months ago. Start working towards your future. We only have a limited time here on earth. It's better to spend time waiting for the opportunity to take action than miss the chance.

"Determine never to be idle. No person will have occasion to complain of the want of time who never loses any. It is wonderful how much can be done if we are always doing." - Thomas Jefferson.

Chapter 32:

How To Deal With Feelings of

Unworthiness

Today we're going to talk about a topic that I hope none of you struggle with. But if you do, I hope to bring some light into your life today. Because i too have had to deal with such feelings before, as recently as a year ago actually.

So before we get into the solutions, we must first understand where these feelings of unworthiness comes form. And we must be aware of them before we can make changes in our lives that brings us out of that state of mind.

Let's start with my life, maybe you will understand the kinds of struggles that I had gone through that led me to feeling unworthy.

Just about 3 years ago, I started my entrepreneurial journey, a journey that was full of excitement and curiousity. After being through a couple of internships at a company, i knew the corporate life wasn't really my thing, and i set out on my own path to making money online... To see if i could find a way to have an income without having to work a 9-5 job. The start was rough as I had no experience whatsoever. But over time i started to find a bit of footing and I made some decent income here and there that would sustain my livelihood for a while. As I was starting to see some success, my "world" came crashing down as something happened with the small business that I had spent almost 3 years building up. And suddenly my income was gone. And I realized I had nothing to show for my 3 years of work. It left me feeling incredibly depressed... Although it doesnt sound like the end of the world to many of you, i felt like i had been set back many years behind my peers who were by then already steadily climbing up the corporate ladder. Feelings that I had made a grave mistake in terms of career choice started creeping up on me. As I tried to figure out what to do with my life, I couldn't help but compare my income to the income that my friends were making. And I felt did feel worthless, and inferior. And I started questioning my whole journey and life choices up till that point.

I started wondering if I was ever going to climb my way back up again, if I would ever figure out how these things actually worked, and all those negative thoughts came day in and out. Eating me alive inside.

It was only after I had done some introspection did I finally started to learn to love myself. And to learn that my journey is unique and mine alone. That I didn't need to, and must not, compare myself to others, did i really start to feel worthy again. I started to believe in my own path, and I felt proud that I had dared to try something that most of my peers were afraid to even try. I found new qualities in myself that I didn't knew I had and I started to forge a new path for myself in my own entrepreneurial journey. Eventually my experience making money online helped me claw my way back up the income ladder, and I have never looked backed since.

For me personally, the one thing that I could take away from my own experience with unworthiness, is to not compare yourself with others. You will never be happy comparing with your peers on income, relationship status, number of friends, number of followers on social media, and all that random things. If you always look at your friends in that way, you will always feel inferior because there will always be someone better than you. Sure you can look to them for inspiration and tips, but never feel that they are superior to you in anyway.. because you are unique in your own beautiful way. You should focus on your own journey and how you can be a better version of yourself. Your peers might have different sets of skills, talents, and expertise, that helped them excel in their fields, but you have your own talents too that you should exploit. You never know what you can achieve until you truly believe in yourself and fully utilise your potential.

For you, your struggle with unworthiness could stem from the way your parents compare you to your siblings, or feeling hopeless trying to find love in this cruel world, or being rejected by companies in your Job applications, or rejection by a potential suitor. These are all valid things that can bring us down. But never let these people tell you what you can or cannot do. Prove to them that you are worthy by constantly improving yourself, mentally, physically, health wise, being emotionally resilient, grow your wisdom, and always love yourself. People cannot love you if you do not love yourself first. That is a quote that i believe very deeply.

No amount of validation from external sources can match the love that I decide to give to myself first.

If you find yourself in situations where you are being bombarded with negativity, whether it be from friends or family, i suggest you take a step back from these people. Find a community where your achievements are celebrated and appreciated, and where you can also offer the same amount of encouragement to others. Join meetup groups in your area with people of similar interests and just enjoy the journey. You will get there eventually if you believe in yourself.

So I challenge each and every one of you to always choose yourself first, look at your own journey as a unique path, different from everybody else, follow your dreams, take action, and never give up. That is the only way to prove to yourself and to the world that you are the most worthy person on the planet.

Chapter 33:

How To Achieve True Happiness

How many of us actually know what happiness really is? And how many of us spend our whole lives searching for it but never seem to be happy?

I want to share with you my story today of how i stumbled upon true happiness and how you can achieve the same for yourself in your life.

Many of us go through the motion of trying to earn money because we think the more money we have, the better our lives will be. We chase the dream of increasing our earning power so that we can afford to buy nicer and more expensive things. And we believe that when we have more money, our happiness level will increase as well and we will be filled with so much money and happiness that we can finally stop chasing it.

Now I just wanna say, Yes, for those who come from a not so affluent background where they have a family to feed and basic needs have to be met to in order for them to survive, having a monetary goal to work towards is truly commendable as their drive, motivation, and sole purpose comes from supporting their family. Their sense of achievement, joy, and happiness comes from seeing their loved ones attaining basic needs and then go on to achieve success later in life at the expense of their time and energy. But they are more than okay with that and they do so with a willing heart, mind, and soul. You might even say that these people have achieved true happiness. Not because they are chasing more money, but because they are using that money to serve a greater purpose other than themselves.

But what about the rest of us who seemingly have everything we could ever want but never seem to be happy? We work hard at our jobs every single day waiting for our next promotion so that we can command a higher pay. And as our income grows, so does our appetite and desire for more expensive material things.

For guys we might chase that fancy new watch like rolex, omega, breitling, drooling over that model that always seem to be on a never-ending waitlist. And as we purchased one, feeling that temporary joy and satisfaction, we quickly look towards that next model as the shiny object we have starts to slowly fade. We lose our so-called happiness in time and We go back to work dreaming about that next watch just to feel that joy and excitement again. This could apply to other material things such as a shiny new technology gadgets smartphones, tv, and even cars.

For women, while might not be true for everyone, They might look towards that designer shoe, that branded handbag, ar that fancy jewellery that costs thousands of dollars to purchase but happily pay for it because they think it makes them feel better about ourselves. Or they could even use these purchases as retail therapy from their stressful lives and jobs.

Whatever these expensive purchases may be, we think that by spend our hard earned money on material things, it will bring us happiness and joy, but somehow it never does, and in most cases it is only temporary satisfactions.

That was exactly what happened with me. I kept chasing a higher income thinking it would bring me happiness. As a lover of technology, I always sought to buy the latest gadgets I could get my hands on. The excitement peaks and then fades. For me I realised that I had created an endless loop of trying to chase happiness but always coming up short.

One day I sat down and reflected on what exactly made me REALLY happy and I started writing down a list.

My List Came down to these in no particular order: Spending time with family, spending time with friends, helping others, having a purpose in life, being at peace with myself, working on my own dreams, singing and making music, exercising, being grateful, and finally being a loving person to others.

As I went through this list, I realised that hey, in none of the list did i write "making more money" or "buying more things". And it finally dawned on me that these are REALLY the things that made me truly happy. And only after I had defined these things did i actively choose to do more of them every single day.

I started spending more quality time with my friends and family, i started playing my favourite sport (Tennis) a few times a week, I chose to be grateful that I can even be alive on this earth, and I chose to be more loving and humble. Finally I also actively chose not to compare myself to people who were more "successful" than I was because comparing yourself to others can NEVER make you happy and will only make you feel inferior when you are not. Always remember that You are special, you are unique, and you are amazing.

After doing these things every single day, I had become a much happier person. It is all about perspective.

So what can you do to achieve happiness for yourself?

I recommend that you do the same thing I did which is to write down a list under the title "When Am I The Happiest?" or "When Was A Time When I Truly Felt Happy?" Start breaking down these memories as you recall your past, and down the essence of the memory. Everybody's list will be different as happiness means different things to every one of us. Once you have your answer, start doing more of these things everyday and tell me how you feel afterwards.

Some days you will forget about what makes you truly happy as you get bombarded by the harsh and cruel things life will throw at you. So I encourage you to put this list somewhere visible where you can see it everyday. Constantly remind yourself of what happiness means to you and shift your mind and body towards these actions every single day. I am sure you will be much happier person after that. See you in the next one :)

Chapter 34:

Overcoming Fear and Self-Doubt

The lack of belief most people have is the reason for their failure at even the smallest things in life. The biggest killer of dreams is the lack of belief in ourselves and the doubt of failure.

We all make mistakes. We all have some ghosts of the past that haunt us. We all have something to hide. We all have something that we regret. But what you are today is not the result of your mistakes.

You are here because of your struggles to make those things go away. You are here now with the power and strength to shape your present and your future.

Our mind is designed to take the shape of what we hold long enough inside it. The things we frequently think about ultimately start filling in the spaces within our memory, so we have to be careful. We have to decide whether we want to stay happy or to hold on to the fear we once wanted to get rid of.

The human spirit and human soul are colored by the impressions we ourselves decide to impose.

The reason why we don't want to explore the possibility of what to do is that subconsciously we don't believe that it can happen for us. We don't believe that we deserve it or if it was meant for us.

So here is something I suggest. Ask yourself, how much time in a day do you spend thinking about your dream? How much time do you spend working on your dreams everyday? What books did you read this year? What new skills have you acquired recently? What have you done that makes you worthy of your dream? Nothing?

Then you are on point with your doubt because you don't have anything to show for when the opportunity presents itself.

You don't succeed because you have this latent fear. Fear that makes you think about the consequences of what will happen if you fail even with all the good things on your hand?

I know that feeling but failure is there to teach you one important and maybe the most essential skill life can teach us; Resilience.

You rediscover your life once you have the strength to fight your every fear and every doubt because you have better things on your hand to care for.

You have another dream to pursue. Another horizon awaits you. Another peak to summit. It doesn't matter if you literally have to run to stand still. You got to do what you got to do, no matter the consequences and the sacrifices.

But failing to do what is required of you has no justifiable defense. Not even fear. Because your fears are self-imposed and you already have many wrong things going on for you right now.

Don't let fear be one of them. Because fear is the most subtle and destructive disease So inhale all your positive energies and exhale all your doubts because you certainly are a better person without them.

Chapter 35:

How To Worry Less

How many of you worry about little things that affect the way you go about your day? That when you're out with your friends having a good time or just carrying out your daily activities, when out of nowhere a sudden burst of sadness enters your heart and mind and immediately you start to think about the worries and troubles you are facing. It is like you're fighting to stay positive and just enjoy your day but your mind just won't let you. It becomes a tug of war or a battle to see who wins?

How many of you also lose sleep because your mind starts racing at bedtime and you're flooded with sad feelings of uncertainty, despair, worthlessness or other negative emotions that when you wake up, that feeling of dread immediately overwhelms you and you just feel like life is too difficult and you just dont want to get out of bed.

Well If you have felt those things or are feeling those things right now, I want to tell you you're not alone. Because I too struggle with those feelings or emotions on a regular basis.

At the time of writing this, I was faced with many uncertainties in life. My business had just ran into some problems, my stocks weren't doing well, I had lost money, my bank account was telling me I wasn't good enough, but most importantly, i had lost confidence. I had lost the ability to face each day with confidence that things will get better. I felt that i was worthless and that bad things will always happen to me. I kept seeing the negative side of things and it took a great deal of emotional toll on me. It wasn't like i chose to think and feel these things, but they just came into my mind whenever they liked. It was like a parasite feeding off my negative energy and thriving on it, and weakening me at the same time.

Now your struggles may be different. You may have a totally different set of circumstances and struggles that you're facing, but the underlying issue is the same. We all go through times of despair, worry, frustration, and uncertainty. And it's totally normal and we shouldn't feel ashamed of it but to accept that it is a part of life and part of our reality.

But there are things we can do to minimise these worries and to shift to a healthier thought pattern that increases our ability to fight off these negative emotions.

I want to give you 5 actionable steps that you can take to worry less and be happier. And these steps are interlinked that can be carried out in fluid succession for the greatest benefit to you. But of course you can choose whichever ones speaks the most to you and it is more important that you are able to practice any one of these steps consistently rather than doing all 5 of them haphazardly. But I want to make sure I give you all the tools so that you can make the best decisions for yourself.

Try this with me right now as I go through these 5 steps and experience the benefit for yourself instead of waiting until something bad happens.

The very first step is simple. Just breathe. When a terrible feeling of sadness rushes into your body out of nowhere, take that as a cue to close your eyes, stop whatever you are doing, and take 5 deep breathes through your nose. Breathing into your chest and diaphragm. Deep breathing has the physiological benefit of calming your nerves and releasing tension in the body and it is a quick way to block out your negative thoughts. Pause the video if you need to do practice your deep breathing before we move on.

And as you deep breathe, begin the second step. Which is to practice gratefulness. Be grateful for what you already have instead of what you think u need to have to be happy. You could be grateful for your dog, your family, your friends, and whatever means the most to you. And if you cannot think of anything to be grateful for, just be grateful that you are even alive and walking on this earth today because that is special and amazing in its own right.

Next is to practice love and kindness to yourself. You are too special and too important to be so cruel to yourself. You deserve to be loved and you owe it to yourself to be kind and forgiving. Life is tough as it is, don't make it harder. If you don't believe in yourself, I believe in you and I believe in your worthiness as a person that you have a lot left to give.

The fourth step is to Live Everyday as if it were your last. Ask yourself, will you still want to spend your time worrying about things out of your control if it was your last day on earth? Will you be able to forgive yourself if you spent 23 out of the last 24 hours of your life worrying? Or will you choose to make the most out of the day by doing things that are meaningful and to practice love to your family, friends, and yourself?

Finally, I just want you to believe in yourself and Have hope that whatever actions you are taking now will bear fruition in the future. That they will not be in vain. That at the end of the day, you have done everything to the very best of your ability and you will have no regrets and you have left no stone unturned.

How do you feel now? Do you feel that it has helped at least a little or even a lot in shaping how you view things now? That you can shift your perspective and focus on the positives instead of the worries?

If it has worked for you today, I want to challenge you to consistently practice as many of these 5 steps throughout your daily lives every single day. When you feel a deep sadness coming over you, come back to this video if you need guidance, or practice these steps if you remember them on your own.

I wish you only good things and I hope that I have helped you that much more today. Thank you for your supporting me and this channel and if you find that I can do more for you, do subscribe to my channel and I'll see you in the next one. Take care.

Chapter 36:

Get Rid of Worry and Focus On The Work

Worry is the active process of bringing one's fears into reality.

Worrying about problems halts productivity by taking your mind off the work in hand.

If you're not careful, a chronic state of worrying can lead you down a dark path that you might find hard to get out of.

Always focus on the required work and required action towards your dream.

Anything could happen, good or bad,

but if you remain focused and do the work despite the problems,

you will through with persistence and succeed.

Always keep your mind on the goal,

your eyes on the prize.

Have an unwavering faith in your abilities no matter what.

Plan for the obvious obstacles that could stand in your way,

but never worry about them until you have to face them.

Tackle it with confidence as they come and move forward with pride.

Problems are bound to arise.

Respond to them necessarily along the way, if they actually happen.

After all, most worries never make it into reality.

Instead focus on what could go right.

Focus on how you can create an environment that will improve your chances of success.

You have the power over your own life and direction.

As children we dreamed big.

We didn't think about all the things that could go wrong.

As children we only saw the possibilities.

We were persistent in getting what we wanted no matter the cost.

As adults we need to be reminded of that child-like faith.

To crush worry as if it were never there.

To only focus on the possibilities.

You cannot be positive and negative at the same time.

You cannot be worrying and hopeful of the future.

You cannot visualise your perfect life while worrying about everything that could go wrong.

Choose one.

Stick to it.

Choose to concentrate on the work.

The result will take care of your worries.

Catch yourself when you feel yourself beginning to worry about things. Instead of dwelling on the problem, choose to double down on the action.

Stay focused and steadfast in the vision of your ultimate goal.

The work now that you must do is the stepping stones to your success.

The work now must have your immediate attention.

The work now requires you to cast worry aside in favour of concentration and focus.

How many stepping stones are you away?

What is next?

Push yourself every single day.

Because only you have the power to create your future.

If not, things will remain the same as they have always been.

Always have a clearly defined goal,

A strong measure of faith,

And an equally strong measure of persistence and grit.

These are the ingredients to creating the life you want.

A life of lasting happiness and success.

Take control instead of accepting things as they are.

Reject anything else that is not the goal that you've set for yourself.

Whatever goal you set, ten times it, and focus on it every day.

The focus will keep your mind on the work until you succeed.

There will be no time to worry when you are too busy taking constant action.

Always have the belief In your heart and soul that you will succeed.
Never let a grain of doubt cast a shadow in your eventual path to victory.

Focus is key to all.
What you focus on, you will create.
Worrying is worse than useless,
it is DETRIMENTAL to your future.

Take control of your thoughts.
When worry pops it's ugly head, force it out with a positive thought of your future.
Don't let the negative illusions of worry live rent-free in your mind.

You are in control here.
Of what you watch,
What you read,
What you listen too
And what you think.

What you think of consistently will become.
Focus on what you want, and how to get there is crucial for lasting happiness and success.

Chapter 37:

Block Out The Critics and Detractors

There is drama everywhere around us. In fact, our whole life is a drama. A drama that has more complex turns and thrillers than the best thriller ever to be made on a cinema screen.

This drama isn't always a result of our own actions. Sometimes we do something stupid to contribute towards anarchy. But mostly the things happening around us seem to be a drama because the critics make a hell out of everything.

We get sucked into things that and someone else's opinions because we do not know what we are doing.

It may sound cliche but remember that it doesn't matter what anyone else says. In fact, most discoveries and inventions got bad press when they were found or made. It was only after they are gone when people actually came to appreciate the true importance of those inventions.

The time will come sooner or later when you are finally appreciated for your work and your effort. But your work should not depend on what others will say.

Your work should not depend on the hope of appreciation or the fear of criticism, rather it should be done because it was meant to be done. You should put your heart and soul in it because you had a reason for all this and only you will reap the fruit, no matter what the world gets from it.

You don't need to do the best out there in the world and neither should you be judged on that standard. But you should put out the best YOU can do because that will someday shut out the critics as they start to see your true potential.

The work itself doesn't matter, but the effort you put behind it does. You don't need to be an insult to anyone who mocks you or criticizes you on even your best work. Empathy is your best approach to bullying.

You cannot possibly shut out every critic. You spend your whole life trying to answer to those meaningless least important people that weren't even able to make their own lives better. Because those who did make something of themselves didn't find it worthwhile to distract and degrade everyone else.

So you should try to spend your time more and more on your good work. Keep a straight sight without even thinking to look at one more ordinary critic who doesn't give a simple feeling of empathy towards your efforts.

You only need to put yourself in others' shoes and look at yourself through their eyes. If you can do that before them, you would have the best reply to any hurtful comment. And that my friend will be true silence.

People always come to gather around you when they see a cause they can relate to. So give them a cause. Give a ray of hope and motivation to people around you and you will finally get to get the critics on your side.

Your critics will help you get to the top from the hardest side there is.

CPSIA information can be obtained
at www.ICGtesting.com
Printed in the USA
LVHW051137120122
708210LV00013B/519